Design by Janet Sieff, Centering Corporation

©2007
All Rights Reserved.
Centering Corporation

ISBN: 1-56123-198-3

Additional copies and other grief resources can be ordered from:
Centering Corporation
PO Box 4600
Omaha, NE 68104

Phone: 866-218-0101

online catalog: www.centering.org
email: centeringcorp@aol.com

How to be a Friend To a Survivor of Suicide

Ask Me...

30 Things I Want You To Know

By Nan Zastrow

Chad Eric Zastrow

Son of Nan and Gary Zastrow

12-04-1971 to 4-16-1993

Because I love him, I remember.

Because I remember, he will never die.

Introduction

A phone call from a long-ago co-worker…
An email from a friend several states away…
An impromptu visit from a stranger who stopped at my office…
A call in the night…
Someone has taken their life…another suicide. And friends are asking questions: "How do I help my friend? What can I possibly say that will take away his or her pain?"

All four of these incidents happened in the same week—and all were unrelated. But, the word has gotten out. People are saying: "She's not afraid to talk about being a survivor of suicide."

Recently, there has been a bizarre increase in suicides, not only in our community, but throughout the nation. And I'm grateful that people—friends of the survivors of suicide—are proactively asking, "What can I do? What shouldn't I do? How can I help?"

Is it possible the taboo is coming out of the closet and people are recognizing that this terrible tragedy called suicide can happen to someone they know? And, it can happen to those you least expect…to the neighbor next door, the physician at the community hospital, the straight "A" student, the model "mom," the elderly lady in a prestigious residential facility, as well as the energetic entrepreneur.

Today, I'm comfortable with being recognized as someone who is willing to talk about suicide and share information based on my own experience. In 1993, this wasn't true. For three years after our own encounter, I lived in the dread of someone asking me about the sudden and unexpected death of my son by suicide. Very few people ventured forward to give encouragement, open the discussion, or even try to understand the impact of this tragedy on our lives. Following Chad's death, a mere ten weeks later, his fiancée took her life, and the cycle repeated itself. Now the nameless taboo hovered over us more than ever.

I remember writing an article about my cloak of shame—feeling accountable for what had happened to my son. I remember placing roses at Jenny's casket (because Chad always bought her roses) and feeling the icy stares of visitors at her wake. I remember being so paranoid about telling strangers how my son died that I would instead ease the conversation by saying it was accidental. I remember going to a different church because I didn't feel comfortable at my own. I remember people changing directions to avoid meeting me face-to-face. I remember the endless sobs, the taunting questions of "Why?," and falling asleep exhausted with my self-imposed misery.

I also vividly remember special people like my family who stood by me with the same love for Chad that I had. They remembered him for who he was—not how he died. I was grateful for Chad's friends who were as mystified as I that this tragedy occurred…and who were there for many years to come, though their lives went on. I remember the brave few in the workplace who broke the code of silence and dared chat a moment, share a memory, or encourage a smile. These were people doing something they felt they had to do though they weren't quite sure if it was right.

Today, the taboo of suicide is gaining attention. The darkness and scorn are being replaced, often reluctantly, by enlightening new views and coping strategies for survivors. The media is more focused than ever on bereaved people (although not always in an appropriate way). Grief, in general, is not hidden from the public. The public accepts that it is real…but just want it to go away as quickly as possible. They use the word "closure" like it really happens.

So, how does it feel to be a survivor of suicide? And how can a friend respond to a suicide survivor with compassion and help them maintain their dignity and self-respect? Here are 30 things I want you to know (based on my personal experience) because it would have helped me.

Immediate Things I Need from You

I am most vulnerable the days preceding the funeral service and for a few weeks after the funeral. The tears are endless, the sadness deep, and the ability to function much impaired. I don't wish to be smothered by your attention, but I need you there when I feel helpless and insecure. I may need you to lead me as a mother may lead a child. I may need you to contact friends because I am so grief-struck that I cannot tell them what has occurred. I may need your shoulder to cry on and your strong arm to hold me up when I am overcome with emotion and self-pity.

I may need you to make notes about all the "important things" I am being told—because minutes from now I will not remember what was said or who told me. I may need you to tell me your name when you come to the wake, because though your face may register familiarity, details escape me. I may need you to call me and remind me to get up in the morning, eat my meals, take my shower, and stick my head outside because I have no energy or desire to move in any direction.

I am a "shell" of the person you once knew. My heart is broken, my spirit weak and my life is shattered. I have no desire to put the pieces back together. Today, I have given in to defeat. I may need you to promise me endlessly that life can go on…and you will be with me every step of the way. I may need you to "walk with me" and never say a word. I may need you to point out the blue sky, the brilliant rainbow, and the softness of sunset. I cannot see the beauty in the world, only the dark night of my soul.

In reality, there may be little you can do to help me. But there is great value in your sustained presence. When I am most vulnerable, here is what I want you to know.

1

Comfort me with your silent presence not with empty words.

Sometimes I just need someone there…letting me know you are available if I want to speak. And other times, I may sit for hours and never say a word. Don't try to soothe me by telling me that "now I have an angel in heaven." Or "he's in a better place." These words don't bring comfort; instead they remind me of the permanency of my loss.

2

Acknowledge my loved one's death.

When you ignore what has happened, you reinforce the stigma of suicide. Pick up the phone. Come to my house. Send a card. Or attend the wake. Show me that you truly care. I know acknowledging this loss is just as uncomfortable for you as it is for me.

3

Give me a hug. Hold my hand.

Pat my shoulder. But, don't tell me you know how I feel. How can you "know" even if you have lost your loved one too? Your gestures shown through the human touch connect more with my soul than words. The time will come when we can share our stories of loss. But for now, I am unique. I stand alone. I am the only one who has ever felt this way.

4

Shelter me from hurtful untruths and gossip.

People talk. Versions of this "misfortune incident" unfold… many with untruths and innuendos that are distorted and spiteful. Stand up, in my defense, and share the opinion that "we do not know what happened or why." When the time is right, the details will be known. For now, respect our family shock and dismay, squelch the gossip. Be a part of the healing not part of the problem. Eventually, I must face these people with the truth.

5

Do not preach God's Word and Plan to me—

Do not imply that I accept this loss without question. I am not ready to embrace my God as my Comforter, yet. I don't understand why He let this happen to me! My relationship with God may be hurting. Right now, I may temporarily have disengaged from God. I fail to remember how "faith…and trust" have brought me through other setbacks or tragedies in my life. I need time to soothe the pain of abandonment that I feel. I will embrace my God as I mend.

6

Don't judge the act of suicide.

I feel ashamed and targeted by the attention this death has caused. I am learning that suicide is a choice that may not always come with a reason. We cannot know the depth of pain or the rationale that preceded one's choice in a nanosecond of time. When you judge him, you judge me. You imply that I was a poor parent (spouse, sibling etc.), that my son suffered mental imbalance, that death was a result of substance abuse or other factors. Don't be so hasty to conclude why this suicide occurred. For months and years, I will live in this shadow of this tragedy and answers may never be sure. Instead of criticism, remind me that God is greater than us and sees far beyond our human understanding and knows His child's soul. God has the power to forgive. I do not blame, I will not feel guilty, I will always believe that my son's choice was not an effort to hurt his family (or friends). My son would want me to be a survivor, not a victim of his choice.

7

Accept my tears, my frustration, and outbursts.

I am fragile and my emotions will erupt. Tears are cleansing and help me release the anxiety I feel. Give me permission to cry, scream, or rant at any given moment. Put your arm around me, hold me, and comfort me because when you can feel my pain…our spirits have become one. If you cannot feel my pain, then how can you expect to be a healing part of my grief?

Needs During the Duration of Intense Grief

Shortly after the funeral, I sense that my friends are unavailable. Suddenly, I am alone with my raw emotions. I felt rejected, abandoned and a struggling lost soul. This period of time may last for months or years—long after others have moved forward making memories in their lives. I feel like I am expected to put on a "happy" face and resume life. Inside I am one person and on the outside—another. I have lost my identity…who am I now? For me, time has stopped. Life has lost its purpose and meaning.

During this period of rehabilitation, I am trying to restore the threads of existence—seeking anything that make sense. I ask questions. I grope for plausible answers. I seek out people, places and things that offer a ray of hope on any dark day. I am afraid of the future…afraid of moving forward and leaving my loved one behind. I see the pity in your face. I hear your words encouraging me to be the person I once used to be. You want me to be "normal" again…and I am helpless in responding to your wishes.

8

Allow me to ask "why?" knowing you don't have the answer either.

This is the beginning of my search for meaning—to make sense out of the senseless. I am overwhelmed with doubt and my mind cannot process any logical explanation why this has happened to me. This question may plague me for years. Though you can't provide answers, you can provide comfort in reiterating that sometimes there aren't acceptable answers to life's events. Let me ask "Why?" until it doesn't matter any more.

9

Help me accept that "it can happen to me."

Tragedies, like this happen to other families, other people... but not to me. I whisper "surely there must be some mistake." I will say these words over and over again with disbelief because I cannot fathom the injustice I feel. I am humbled by my grief. With your gentle hug and kind voice, let me know that you can't believe it either. This will comfort me that the "surprise" I feel was also felt by you.

10

Respect my feelings of guilt.

The "shoulda's, woulda's, and coulda's" are gnawing at my conscience. "If only" I had seen it coming…things might be different. "What did I do wrong?" Allow me time to work through these issues in my mind and feel sorry for my powerlessness to change the outcome of this event. Help me to accept that things beyond my control influenced his decision and his death was his ultimate sacrifice in his loss of hope.

11

Respect my anger and fear; don't negate it.

There are times I might feel hostile and angry. Anger is a symbol of love that says, "I cared." I feel like an outsider looking in. I'm angry with God, the media, my child (the victim), his friends, and myself for allowing this tragedy to happen. Allow me to demonstrate my anger because I deserve the right to express my feelings. I cannot see beyond the "black hole" that cradles the emptiness of my soul. Help me channel my anger in non-threatening ways; but should my approach hint of self-harm or harm to someone else, urge me to seek professional intervention.

12

Help me trust again.

To trust is to put confidence in you that you will respect my pain and not abandon me. I trusted my loved one and was hurt. I gave love unconditionally and was betrayed. Now I must learn to forgive and trust again. When I open my heart to you, I trust that you are sincere and concerned. Don't make promises you cannot keep. If you say you are coming or promise to call, I will wait for you. Act in a way that exemplifies your code of ethics for life and then ask yourself…"Am I someone she can trust?"

13

Be patient as I struggle to answer the inevitable questions.

When I am asked, "How many children do you have?" Help me answer without hesitation that "I have two, but one has died." When someone asks, "How did he die?," give me the courage to answer honestly and briefly without regret. Help me to bear the pitiful looks of those who wish they had not asked and educate them by letting them know, it doesn't make any difference how he died, what matters is…he died.

14

**Trust that I am not crazy,
but respect the mysteries of grief.**

Grief brings mysteries that comfort a few and baffle many. Did I hear his voice on the phone? Was there a message in that dream? Did I see his face in a crowd? Can I really sense his presence in an empty room? Did I hear his voice, smell his cologne, feel a whisper of a kiss on my cheek? I am not crazy. I am normal with grief. These paranormal events bring comfort to me in knowing his spirit lives on.

15

Understand the intensity of my healing.

Healing grief is physical, emotional, mental, spiritual; and therefore, consuming. I'm accepting that I will not heal from this pain unless I face my loss and take positive steps to embrace it. Be patient on days when I move forward one step and on another day take two steps back. Knowing you understand, will bring me closer to resolving this conflict within.

16

Show me that it is okay to accept support and help from someone who cares.

I was independent and strong. Now I feel humble and weak. My pride tells me that I don't need you. But my spirit yearns for the comfort of your voice, the touch of your hand, and the empathy you radiate. Let me trust. Let me grasp the concept of accepting "help" from someone else when I feel compelled to "do this alone." Be my strength. Be my courage and lead me gently forward.

17

Share your stories
but understand my hesitation.

When you talk about your child (husband, parent i.e.), I may seem distant or uninterested. That's because it hurts to remember that I may never have those precious intimate experiences that give you joy. In your joy I feel a whimper of my self-pity for dreams that will never be fulfilled. In time, I will feel comfortable sharing your stories of life, but for now it hurts. However, do not shelter me from your sharing for I must learn to live in the real world with the experiences of others and build new dreams of my own.

18

Give me an opportunity for humor.

Although someone's tragic misfortune in life is not something to laugh about, there is a healing affect in humor. My conscience tells me " you are grieving…you should not laugh," but my spirit yearns for some sense of relief that comes with a timely chuckle, a humorous story about my loved one, or a short escape in a humorous movie or television show. Remind me that it is okay to "laugh." Laughter emanates healing promises and reminds me that life can be "fun" again.

19

Encourage my return to "routine" and to put structure back into my life.

The need to restore routine is essential. This pattern of "normalcy" fills the hours of my day with "other" thoughts and activities. Accompany me on social outings until I am comfortable to go alone (i.e. church, health club, shopping, sports). I may need to go slowly at first—perhaps an hour or two at a time. Being accepted by those in a social situation will give me the confidence that I still "belong."

20

**Help me adjust to the task
of returning to the workplace.**

Going to work doesn't mean my grief is over. It means I wish to replace the endless hours of grief and return to an environment of people I know. I return to the workplace with fears: "Can I be productive?" "How will I focus my attention on my job?" My tears fall without warning. I am worried about losing my job because I cannot concentrate on the tasks before me. I want you to treat me just like you did before—but give me time to feel comfortable again. Don't isolate me for fear of causing tears. I need to share my tears and my pain; and I want you to be a part of my healing.

21

Encourage me to maintain my personal health.

It's easy to minimize personal health, get adequate rest, and ignore symptoms of physical illness. In the throes of grief, it's easy to forget to eat or eat too much. I may give the impression that I don't care, but I do not wish to fight a battle with disease caused by neglect. Encourage me to find life balance, that includes diet, exercise, and rest. These will strengthen me physically and allow my inner spirit to emerge.

22

Allow me the "greed" of holding on before letting go.

Don't tell me "life goes on"…too soon. Let me experience this for myself and gradually, gently let go of the ties that bind. But don't let me get "stuck in time" where grief becomes a way of life and me its victim. When I am ready to let go, you will know. Be there to welcome me and show me the possibilities that await my reluctant heart. I may "let go," but I will not forget.

Support me as I Heal

As the world turns and the days slip by, I forever carry my precious loss close to my heart. I am a survivor. I am healing. I am triumphant. But, I am forever changed. Grief is not forgotten, but lives quietly in the heart and loudly in the memories. Good grief finds recovery, but never resolution. A recovering griever learns to live with the pain like the alcoholic learns to live without drink. There is always the yearning to go backward and capture the moments that once seemed magical.

23

**Stay connected.
I need your help long after the funeral.**

I may give the signal that I don't need any "help" by refusing your invitations and by isolating myself from those who care for me. But inside, my heart is breaking. I will need help for many months or years to come. Be gentle but persistent. Work your way into my shattered life through simple gestures of caring like a phone call, an impromptu short visit or bringing the family a baked treat. Allow me respite by offering to entertain the children, walk the dog, or give me time alone. Be there when others walk away.

24

Comfort me with the gift of memories.

Memories may be painful, but I need to speak his name, tell his story, and cherish the memories of this person—so precious to me. Don't fear telling me the stories of my loved one or speaking his name. I need to know that you remember him just as I do. I need to know that he touched someone else's life with his smile, his laugh, his antics, his words, or his contagious zest for life. Show me pictures of "good days" and these will remind me that he lives within me through the gift of memories.

25

Remember me on special days.

When celebration days bring you joy, remember that I struggle to face them. The celebration of a birthday, Christmas, Mother's Day, and other religious and public holidays have a different meaning for me now. They are reminders of the way it was and I must find a new way to weave them into my life without regrets. A full calendar of anniversary dates may not be enough to heal my pain. I must experience each one in my own way and every season will have its own hardships. A card, a flower, a phone call and a pleasant word will let me know that you have not forgotten my loss and you share my pain.

26

Expect recovery, but never closure.

There will be setbacks. Be patient with me; healing takes time. As I begin recovery, I may appear full of hope one day; and the next, wonder if I will ever be "me" again. Don't think, "She should be over it by now." The process of grieving is a way to work through my feelings and frustrations, but there is no such thing as closure. I will forever live with my loss, but I can recover in ways that make this a part of my life's experience that help me personally grow.

27

Help me find ways to say good-bye.

The suddenness of this death has left me struggling with the thoughts of unfinished business. If only I had said, "I love you" one more time. I want to bring back the precious moments of our last time together when things were "right." Remind me that saying good-bye can be achieved through ritual. Also remind me that someday we will meet again and say "hello."

28

Help me find peace in ritual.

Show me ways to satisfy my need of honoring his memory. A simple candle lit on a special day, a visit to the cemetery, a donation in his memory…and other worthy ways to give me that "feel good" euphoria. It helps me to accept this his life mattered – and every life serves a purpose. Peace is the silence of life surrounded with love and the hush of knowing, "it's okay."

29

Accept that normal for me is "new."

I will not be the person I once was. My dreams are altered. My priorities have changed. I am struggling to identify the emerging person that I will become. I cannot go back to they way I used to be, but I believe that the person I can become is better, stronger, wiser, and more compassionate than ever imaginable. Love me for who I am now for I must step from the shadow of my grief and stand in the rays of hope.

30

Give me hope...
the belief that things will be better again.

In the shadow of a mending heart, it is difficult to see the sunshine streaming through. Hope comes with small miracles every day. Help me envision hope through a day without tears, the companionship of a new friend, a song of peace and healing, the opportunity to try something new, and in countless ways that signify positive change. Hope is obtainable, hope is the product of attitude. Teach me to find the "good" in everything I do. Demonstrate hope through true friendship...for then I know that because you cared, I can go on.

You will know when I have stumbled upon the "one thing" that allows me to live life as "me" again. I will wear a smile. I will have new dreams. I will tell my story with a sparkle in my eyes that reminds me I need never forget. I will not hide. Challenges in life have tested me. I have grown through my journey. I will emerge as someone new. I will be known as a survivor.

1. Comfort me with your silent presence not with empty words.
2. Acknowledge my loved one's death.
3. Give me a hug, hold my hand.
4. Shelter me from hurtful untruths and gossip.
5. Do not preach God's word and plan to me.
6. Don't judge the act of suicide.
7. Accept my tears, my frustration, and outbursts.
8. Allow me to ask "why?" knowing you don't have the answer.
9. Help me accept that "it can happen to me."
10. Respect my feelings of guilt.
11. Respect my anger and fear; don't negate it.
12. Help me trust again.
13. Be patient as I struggle to answer the inevitable questions.
14. Trust that I am not crazy, but respect the mysteries of grief.
15. Understand the intensity of my "grief work."
16. Show me that it is okay to accept support and help from someone who cares.
17. Share your stories but understand my hesitation.
18. Give me an opportunity for humor when appropriate.
19. Encourage my return to "routine" and to put structure back into my life.
20. Help me adjust to the task of returning to the workplace.
21. Encourage me to maintain my personal health.
22. Allow me to "greed" of holding on before letting go.
23. Stay connected.
24. Comfort me with the gift of memories.
25. Remember me on special days.
26. Expect recovery, but never closure.
27. Help me find ways to say good-bye.
28. Help me find peace in ritual.
29. Accept tht normal for me is "new."
30. Give me hope... the belief that things will be better again.

About the Author

"I always wanted to write," said Nan Zastrow. "But I never dreamed it would be about death, grief, and mourning." Today I write to heal my pain and teach others that even after a life-changing event, there can be a reason and a purpose to go on living."

On April 16, 1993, Chad Zastrow, the son of Nan and Gary died as the result of suicide. Ten weeks later Chad's fiancée took her life. This double tragedy inspired the Zastrows to create a ministry of hope. They formed a non-profit organization called ©Roots and Wings (Wings™ is a trademark of ©Roots and Wings, Ltd.) They published the Wings™ magazine for the bereaved and caregivers from 1993 through 2003. The magazine was composed of inspiration, hope, and true stories about people coping with grief. In July 2003, Nan began writing for *Grief Digest*. In 2004, the Wings non-profit organization refocused its efforts as a grief education ministry with the purpose of "Honoring the Past and Rebuilding the Future."

Nan and Gary are certified grief educators through the Center for Loss and Life Transition in Colorado. Through workshops, seminars, and group presentations, Nan and Gary create community awareness about the grief experience. Wings™ hosts an annual Spring Seminar with a professional speaker and an annual *When the Holiday Hurts* workshop with a unique theme-based program each year. They also offer education and support groups 3-4 times each year.

Nan is the author of a book, ***Blessed Are They That Mourn*** (Available through Centering Corp.) and over forty Editor's Journal Articles in *Wings*™, *Grief Digest* and other publications. Nan has also published 3 Holiday Programs for the Bereaved titled: ***The Legend of the Ebber, Taming the Holiday Blues, and Something Old, Something New, Something Just to Get You Through.*** These are available on their website: www.wingsgrief.org.

For additional copies contact Centering Corporation:
online catalog: www.centering.org
email: centeringcorp@aol.com